You can't put sh
For floating and
A fish needs to swish.

A bird doesn't wear a fancy dress.
A bird in a dress makes a big mess.

A tie on a snake? Where would it go?
He'd wiggle out of it, don't you know?

You don't need a jacket for these goats.
They're already wearing winter coats.

There's just no use begging or crying.
Pigs don't wear socks,
So you better stop trying.

A crab gets crabby if dressed in lace.
She waves her arm to hide her face.

Would you put shoes on a horse?
Yes, if he jogged on a race course.

Animals don't like to be dressed up.
Instead,
They like to be petted, hugged,
and fed!